Could You Walk in *Their* Shoes?

Sharita Emerson Bell

Together with Love, LLC
Nashville, TN 37207

Publisher: Together with Love, LLC
Project Manager: Sedrik Newbern, Newbern Consulting, LLC
Editor: Linda Wolf, Network Publishing Partners, Inc.
Cover Designer: M Hurley, Teknigram Graphics, Inc.

Disclaimer

This is a work of authorship that is based upon the author's personal experiences. However, no names have been used, and in order to maintain anonymity, the author may have changed some identifying characteristics and details such as physical properties, occupations, and places of the events.

Cover photo: Whitney Russell

Printed in the United States of America
First Edition: May 2021

ISBN Paperback: 978-0-578-88861-3

Library of Congress Control Number: 2021906861

I dedicate this book to:

My husband: Thank you for loving and supporting me through the many stages of this book.

My son: Thank you for allowing me to drag you to my school activities for most of your life. So proud of you.

My mom and sister: Thank you for being the two queens in my life and loving me unconditionally.

To my heavenly granny: Thank you for your never-ending nurturing.

Introduction

Life can be hard when you have ***all*** your needs and wants met. Imagine being an inner-city student without the basic necessities such as love, attention, support, money, transportation, food, housing, and/or parent(s)—all before the age of 10, while still expected to be a productive student.

I wrote this book as a call to action. For whom? To all educators, college students, community members, and corporations. There is a growing group of students in this country who desperately need our ongoing help.

It's not enough to hear about inner-city students—it's best to take a walk in their shoes. Afterwards, you may conclude that they need *education majors* to understand and learn their experiences and backgrounds; *teachers and administrators* to support, respect, and treat them with equity; *community members* to become mentors academically and spiritually; and *corporate sponsors* to build strong partnerships to help with local funding and career success.

Help me in spreading their story...

Could You Walk in *Their* Shoes?

Stories

No Response

She cried on my shoulder for what seemed like hours, but it lasted only two minutes. As the fourth grader regained her composure, she told me behind her tears that her mother had been shot by robbers in the leg as she slept. After the student heard the gunshots, she and her siblings ran upstairs to see blood and meat, as she described, on the wall. The student told me that her dad arrived upstairs moments later to report that the robbers ran out the back door.

I was so hurt by my student's story that I could do nothing but continue to listen and let her express her anger, sadness, and fear.

After about three days, she once again appeared in my office. I asked her how she was doing, and she informed me that she was transferring because she had to go live with her aunt. With her head hung low, she also told me that it was her dad who shot her mom. My heart sank.

I thought to myself, how do you deal with such disheartening news about your mother, but deal with angry feelings toward your father, whom you love as well. I told her she could always call me if she needed to talk and that I would miss her. I never heard from her again and often wondered how her life changed and how she was adapting.

Lesson of the Day: Every incident doesn't need a response or explanation. Sometimes a student just needs a shoulder to cry on.

Reflection: A lot of times, we as the adults do more of the talking and less of the listening. A student in need of consoling should leave feeling as though a weight has been lifted, not feeling like they just left an "it-will-be-okay" lecture. Maybe use a couple guiding questions if you must engage, however still allow the student to talk (i.e., "How does that make you feel?"). Stay away from questions like, "What happened?" and "Why?" until the student is ready. You can learn a lot about a student and build a trusting relationship if you let them speak on their terms.

The Coat

Whispers could be heard echoing throughout the hallway as the parent wore "the coat" into the building. Who will say something to her? Why is she wearing it? What is she thinking? Those were the questions being asked every time we saw the parent wearing "the coat."

After about two weeks, as the school counselor, I felt it was my duty to address this parent and her rather odd coat. Not knowing if she would "go off" on me, I finally gained enough nerve to nicely confront her about the breast with nipples drawn in permanent black marker on her light-colored jacket.

I informed her that the coat was inappropriate to wear in our school building around students. In addition, I asked her what reason she had for wearing such a coat. She informed me that someone had broken into her house and stolen her clothes, and that was the only coat she had. Who am I to judge someone's reason for wearing a booby coat to school?

So, I replied, "If I buy you another coat, will you not wear that coat anymore?" She said, "Yes." I kept my word and bought her a nice fur hooded coat, but there was one catch—she had to hand over the booby coat.

Lesson of the Day: Don't be afraid to do your job even if you think you may be met with a little opposition. You're built for it.

Reflection: Parents can often be intimidating, but remember, you are there to serve the students. That means, if you must confront a parent, there are tactful ways of doing so. For example, approach a parent with confidence. If you are approaching a parent in a timid or shy manner, they may feel like they can lead the conversation. Second, stay calm and professional. If a parent has an attitude and you lose your cool, it may end with you being reprimanded, and your efforts could be wasted.

Sight Words

The teacher threw open my office door and handed me what appeared to be a normal blue folder. After I opened it, my mouth literally flew open with shock. Inside the folder were remnants of a singed piece of paper that used to be the student's sight words. The first grader's mom had set his sight words on fire. Why? Because she had told the teacher not to send any more homework home because she (the mother) could not do it.

After I closed my mouth, I immediately got on the phone and called DCS.* The police arrived, took a picture of the folder, and left in disbelief. The next day, the same first grader came to school with the skin of his thumb tattered. He said his mother did it. That was it!!!

Again, I called DCS and the police; however, this time I threatened to call the mayor's office if they did not reprimand this mother. Both showed up after school. The police paid the mother a visit, and DCS kept the student after school until an investigation into the mother's bizarre behavior took place.

*Department of Child Services

Lesson of the Day: You are your students' biggest advocate. Be persistent until your voice is heard.

Reflection: A lot of times in situations that involve some sort of abuse, the ball often gets dropped because there is no follow-up. As your students' advocate, one of your biggest responsibilities should be making sure your students are not harmed in any way. Following the correct protocol for suspected abuse is a must. Afterwards, making sure actions were implemented is even more important.

4, 8, and 10

Three siblings, ages 4, 8, and 10, showed up at school well after the school year had started. I asked what school they had transferred from. The answer: None. Next question—Were they from a third world country? The answer: No.

"Okay, where do they live?" I asked. The answer: Across the street. Last question—have they been homeschooled? You guessed the answer: No.

They walked into our school looking like deer in headlights, for they had never attended a school before. They didn't talk; they just stared. My first reaction was anger!!! How could parents keep their kids hidden away from society this long? This was the worst case of educational neglect I and others had ever seen.

Technically, they were all at a Pre-K level. They didn't know their numbers or letters. Heck, they didn't even know how to hold a pencil. The decision was made to place them all one grade behind their age group. The 4-year-old had the best chance of being on grade level academically than the others since she was starting out in Pre-K.

Although the students had a long road ahead of them, with testing from the school psychologist and caring teachers who were nurturing, they would have a chance to become educated productive citizens, although possibly learning-delayed. Our hope was that the three younger siblings at home (yes, I said the three younger siblings at home) would have a better chance at starting out in school.

Lesson of the Day: Don't judge—teach. Every kid deserves the right to an education.

Reflection: We don't always know why parents make the decisions they make. Again, it is not our place to judge. However, when it comes to children, it is our duty as educators to provide students with a free public education no matter the family circumstances. In many instances with inner-city students, school is the safest, most nurturing environment they know... a place where there are caring adults and a hot meal. At the end of the school year, most students are excited about the summer. However, you will find that there are quite a few students who don't want school to end due to the lack of the home essentials and care needed for a happy summer break.

An Angel

She was a beautiful brown little girl with a demeanor that exuded the spirit of God. We were told that the kindergartner had cancer—a brain tumor. She went to her chemo treatments every Tuesday and was out on Wednesdays because the treatments made her weak; however, she was back on Thursdays. I would often go sit in her class just to watch the strength that this little soul displayed. And, with permission from her parents, I would take her for ice cream. Watching her always made me think, if this baby could come to school while having cancer and having to endure Lord only knows how much pain, I had no room to complain.

As her chemotherapy became more intense, she had to be hospitalized. Oh, how I missed her at school. I would go to visit her at the hospital and play dress-up or just color with her. Not too long after first grade began, she built up her strength to start school, but then she suffered an aneurysm and did not recover. To this very day, I am still close with the family because being around them gives me a little piece of her.

Lesson of the Day: This is not only a job, but a ministry. Some relationships formed may last a lifetime. God, thank you for sharing your special gift with us. I miss you, my little angel.

Reflection: There are students who cross your threshold that you never forget. Instead of becoming their hero, they become yours. In such instances, allow yourself to learn from them. God sends angels in many forms. It's okay to form genuine and pure relationships with your students. Some spirit-led missions are meant to go beyond the classroom.

The Gift of Giving

Each year during the Christmas holiday, local churches, sports teams, and nonprofit organizations blessed our students. However, this particular year, blessings seemed to rain upon our school. Local firefighters decided to gift every student in our school with a brand-new coat for the winter…nice warm coats too. In addition, a national brand company based in the city gave **each** student a pair of shoes (hence, the cover picture) along with a bundle of socks and a hat.

It was a beautiful sight to see—men and women in a huge circle sitting on stools putting little feet in the metal shoe-measuring device, sizing kids for brand new shoes. I've never witnessed the gift of giving in such an amazing, heartfelt way.

And, please don't think for a second that these children weren't appreciative. Students were walking around with the biggest smiles on their faces while trotting around with their classmates. That day, I was blessed to witness true acts of selflessness…more concern for the needs and wishes of others.

Lesson of the Day: If you are able, don't pass up the opportunity to give. When you give from the heart, you receive a greater gift to the heart.

Reflection: Oftentimes, we spend so much of our money giving to people who have just as much as we do during the holidays. However, if you want to experience pure joy, spread love and kindness to those less fortunate than you. Moreover, if you spend time and/or money giving to those who are truly in need, you will experience a strong sense of physical, economic, and social well-being that will keep you in the spirit of giving all year long.

The Babysitter

The 10-year-old fifth grader was babysitting her 4-year-old sister and her baby niece, the child of her 18-year-old big sister. Their mom was in jail and the fifth grader lived with her big sister. As her big sister decided to go out partying that night, leaving my student with the little ones, gun shots rang throughout the neighborhood in the late-night hours.

Terrified, the 10-year-old called her big sister only to hear through the phone, "Don't call this phone no (bleep, bleep) more!" As they continued to wait, they saw a rat. The little babysitter decided to call her grandmother, who had no transportation. "Just run upstairs, go to your room and put a towel under the door," the grandmother advised her granddaughter.

At school the next day, the fifth grader could not concentrate. She was easily angered and agitated and cried when the teacher asked her to get in line. After being sent to me and letting me know of her horrific night, I began to console her as well as question her. She was really scared and told me not to tell her big sister that she had talked with me.

As I began to probe, I found out that at her last school, her big sister was questioned about some bruises that the fifth grader had. I asked her if she had any bruises this time, and to my surprise, she said yes and showed them to me. After I called and reported the abuse and neglect, the child and her sister were removed from the home that day to live with their grandmother.

Lesson of the Day: Do not ignore signs of distress. Most students have a reason why they act the way they do. It's not always easy to identify; however, asking the right questions in the right manner will get your students to open up.

Reflection: Educators must turn from possible rigid ways and squeeze time in for social and emotional learning (SEL). Lots of students aren't aware that they don't yet understand how to manage their emotions. Younger students don't always have the capability to verbalize how they feel. Some tend to shut down or lash out when they're feeling depressed or stressed. Because such behaviors can be misconstrued as negative attitudes, it is imperative that educators incorporate time in their daily schedule, perhaps first thing in the morning (at morning meeting), to allow for students to start a positive day and express themselves in a safe environment. In doing so, students tend to focus and have a better outlook on their day and their school year.

Magician

Day after day, she would lie on her mat disturbing other Pre-K students because she refused to take a nap. As I did my rounds, some days just dropping into classrooms, I noticed that this student was all over her mat making noises and keeping other students from sleeping. The teacher asked me what I could do to help. She told me she had tried everything from promising her treats to extra free time.

I asked the little student to come with me to my office. As we entered my office, I was praying for an idea. I saw a cute little bear sitting up on my bookshelf. I began to tell the student that my poor baby bear was really sleepy and needed a nap. I asked her if I let her take him downstairs, would she allow my bear to nap with her?

After she agreed, I took the preschooler back to class and she laid down as I placed the bear right beside her and put the blanket on them both. The teacher called me minutes later and said, "Are you a magician or something?" She then went on to tell me how her little student had come back to the classroom and gone straight to sleep.

Lesson of the Day: When in doubt...pray. God will give an answer. Just make your request known and He will hear you.

Reflection: Many educators are really hard on themselves because they think they can "fix" their students. Although it is a gift for many to be educators, it doesn't mean we can always do it alone. Not only do we have to call on colleagues for professional opinions, but also on a higher being for guidance. When you pray for answers, you are acknowledging that you need help. And, if you ask for help, it shall be given to you.

You Saved My Baby

She was an odd student. She never gave us eye contact, her hair was never combed, and she appeared to stumble as she walked. After being referred to me, I began to establish a relationship with the 12-year-old. Her innocence was delightful as I listened to her accent that was a cross between Dorothy of the *Wizard of Oz* and Celia from *The Color Purple*. As time went on, other staff members began to comb her hair and buy her clothes.

As our relationship grew, I learned that she had been taken away from her biological mother and placed with her father at the age of 2. One day, the student came to me complaining about her leg. She had been kicked. After further questioning, she began to divulge the physical abuse she was experiencing.

The police arrived to question the student and after a few responses from her, I could see the policeman's eyes water. After she left the room, the policeman said, "I know that child is not lying. She doesn't have the capability to make up a lie... she is so innocent."

Eventually, DCS got involved, and she was removed from the home of her alcoholic father and placed with his 90-year-old grandmother who suffered from dementia. Of course, that did not work out. The student walked off while in her great-grandmother's care, which prompted a search team. She was then removed from her great-grandmother's home.

Before placing her into foster care, DCS tried one more time to find family members. They decided to place her with her maternal grandmother who the student had not seen in a while and grant visitation to her biological mother who she hadn't seen since she was 2 years old. I asked and was granted permission to take her to be reunited with her maternal family. Overwhelmingly excited, with every passing mile, she would look out the window and ask, "Are we there yet?"

As we pulled up to the house, a sober lady who identified herself as her mom, came out of the house with watery eyes and slowly approached the student. She kissed her all over her face and hugged her while she cried tears of joy. As I looked off with tears in my eyes, she turned to me and repeated softly, "You saved my baby, you saved my baby."

Lesson of the Day: When everyone works together, miracles happen.

Reflection: In today's world, education goes beyond reading, writing, and arithmetic. It took a village to make sure this student was ready for school, allowing her to have a successful day without being subject to criticism and bullying. It is our job to work for her on the inside while agencies, such as DCS, work for her on the outside.

The Bead

The student walked up to the teacher, holding his throat. He uttered the words, "I can't breathe." After the nurse checked him out and discovered he could breathe, we called his dad. While we waited for his dad to come, we began to ask him more questions on why he felt like he couldn't breathe.

He told us that during class, he put a small object in his mouth and while coming down the steps of the school, he tripped and swallowed it. His dad came in very angrily and told him he had no business sticking anything in his mouth. I told the dad that he needed to take him to the emergency room to get him checked because, although the student could breathe, he still looked distressed.

The next day the mom called us to let us know that the dad took his son to the doctor. They found something lodged in his throat and he had to have emergency surgery.

Lesson of the Day: Listen to your child/student. It is better to be safe than live with regret.

Reflection: These days, children are looked upon as mini adults because they have so many adult-like responsibilities. However, children do silly things—that's why they are "children." They must learn from their mistakes just like we did. In doing so, adults must give them wiggle room to grow. All situations can't be controlled; however, we must be there for them when they fall. That means listening and showing patience, not physical and/or verbal abuse. It is critical that each action have a positive reaction. In doing so, lives can be saved in more ways than one.

The Doctor's Office

The teacher called me saying, "Come and get her!" As I entered the classroom, the fourth grader was actually sitting in her locker holding her knees. After talking to her for a minute, she finally grabbed my hand so I could lead her to my office. The student had some emotional issues and had not been on her medicine for some time.

I volunteered to take her to the doctor since a release form was signed by her mother who could not make the appointment. Sitting there in the doctor's office with a student who was not my child was awkward. What if they asked me questions about her that only a parent would know? I was a little nervous. As the doctor asked me a series of questions about her moods, surprisingly I could answer them. That's how much time I had vested in this student.

After the appointment, I drove to the pharmacist, got her medicine, and gave it to the school nurse to administer. What a wonderful rest of the school year she had. She was focused in her classes and her behavior improved tremendously. As the year ended, I was on the stage during the fourth-grade graduation ceremony to give handshakes. When her name was called, she glanced over at me and began sobbing. She hugged me tight with gratitude like a child would hug her mom, and I held her tight to let her know how proud I was… like a mom. As the audience saw tears flow down my cheeks, they knew they had witnessed something special.

Lesson of the Day: Sometimes we must go beyond our scope as educators to make a major impact on our students.

Reflection: As educators, you have a choice how much you are willing to do beyond your job description for your students. If it makes you feel uncomfortable, then don't do it. However, in your line of work, you must remember why you chose to be a teacher, counselor, social worker, administrator, school psychologist, or any career working with children. Was it for the paycheck? Was it because your parent was a teacher? Or, was it because you wanted to make a difference in your students' lives? If your answer was making a difference, then it may entail stepping out of your comfort zone to produce positive outcomes.

Beauty Set

She loved "Hello Kitty" and asked me for something the whole year. For her birthday, I finally got her a "Hello Kitty" beauty set with a mirror, hair bows, barrettes, and other items.

After a while, I asked her how she was enjoying her gift. She told me that upon the request of her mother, she was to wrap it up and give it to her younger sister for Christmas. Of course, my initial reaction (to myself) was, "What...are you serious? *I* put time and effort into finding the perfect gift for my student to enjoy!"

Then, I had to stop and realize something...in this line of work, you must constantly remind yourself, it's not about you. I had to get her something else and keep it moving because no matter what, I was still a blessing to her.

Lesson of the Day: Sometimes things don't go as planned, and it's still okay.

Reflection: When working in inner-city schools, you don't know what parents are facing at home. Instead of a child getting a cake for their birthday, maybe a bill must get paid to keep the lights on. When you do something for students, know that although your intentions may be good, priorities may be different in their home. In this line of work, you can't take situations personally. You must continue to help where you can and hope that it turns out for the best.

Flagpole

It had been a good day. The school bell rang for dismissal and the kindergartners were called first. As I stood on my post for dismissal and watched the third and fourth graders walk out the door, I began to see students and teachers run back to the building. When I ran out to see what was going on, they yelled, "They're shooting!"

The gun shots were so close to the kids at the flagpole, you could smell the gun powder. Without thinking, teachers began grabbing students as fast as they could. Students were afraid as they were being swept up without any explanation. The school immediately went into lockdown. After parents got the word that there was a shooting, they quickly ran to the school. Parents weren't allowed to enter the building to get their kids and no one could exit.

Parents became very upset; however, we had to wait until the police cleared it with our principal to abort the lockdown. At that moment, it really hit home that people would put innocent lives in harm's way for their own selfish desires. That day, if nothing else, students left school knowing their teachers were there for them.

Lesson of the Day: Loco Parentis…you are there in the absence of the parent. It's up to you to keep every student safe, at all times, at any cost.

Reflection: Research has shown that living near a violent neighborhood takes its toll on children. Students who are exposed to trauma often have feelings of depression and stress and more than likely experience some form of PTSD (Post Traumatic Stress Disorder). When we take on the role of educators, one of our main duties is the responsibility for the health, safety, and welfare of the children we serve. It is a huge undertaking, and sometimes an even bigger challenge than what we signed up for. However, we must remember that when parents leave the school building, they are essentially entrusting us to stand in "loco parentis," assuming the responsibility of protecting their children like we would our own.

Bus Ride

I heard the ambulance pull up to the school. A student was having an asthma attack. She was very scared and wanting her mom. Our principal made the administrative decision to have the student transported to the hospital while contacting her mother. A staff member volunteered to ride with the student in the ambulance and I volunteered to pick the staff member up from the hospital. When I got to the hospital to pick up the other teacher, she told me we could not leave until the mom showed up. I said okay, and we proceeded to wait.

After quite some time, I thought to myself, "What type of mom doesn't show up when her child has been sent to the emergency room?" After we waited over an hour trying to keep the little girl occupied, her mother suddenly burst through the door. She told us she didn't have a car and had to take the bus from work, which probably included a transfer because she worked far from the hospital.

Lesson of the Day: Don't assume anything about the population you serve. You don't know their story.

Reflection: You will find that if you sit down with most inner-city parents, they are doing the best they can with what they have. Most of the parents are working long hours at low-paying jobs trying to make ends meet.

When you presume that all low-income families are just sitting at home drawing welfare, you are stereotyping and setting yourself up for not only making assumptions, but possibly mistreating students based on what you think is going on in their home.

The Note

I was watching the news when I heard that a kindergarten student in our neighborhood was shot while sitting on his porch. All night long I worried, hoping and praying it wasn't one of our students. As soon as I walked in the doorway of the school the next morning, I was told that it was, in fact, one of our students. He was sitting on the porch playing when a bullet grazed his head in the crossfire.

After hearing such horrific news, I immediately ran to the teacher to inform her. While standing there talking to his teacher, the student who had been shot walked through the door still wearing his hospital band from the night before. As we ran to him in complete disbelief, he stood quietly and handed us a note. It read that if he complained of his head hurting, we were to call the number listed.

I was completely shocked and angry. How could you send a kid to school which such trauma? Even if nothing appeared wrong with him, I would have kept my child home the next day to make sure he was okay. I brought him up to my office to play with my toy cars and gave him lots of attention. While giving him a hug, he uttered these words I will never forget, "I not die." At that moment I just thanked God he was still with us. Later that day, his teacher had to call the number listed on the note because his head began to hurt.

Lesson of the Day: Sometimes there isn't a lesson. Just be still and know that He is God.

Reflection: As school counselors, you are taught how to have a comprehensive program that focuses on the needs of the students but not on your personal emotions. Oftentimes, events happen so fast, you almost become desensitized to the sorrow associated with your job. When you start to feel overwhelmed, it is okay to take a mental health day...that is true with any job. No one is going to take care of you, but you. It takes some people years before they gain an understanding of self-care to discover they're totally burnt out. Take a day or two, be still, and pray. Rejuvenate yourself and come back renewed.

Taught Lesson for Whom?

The third grader tore up the principal's office as she threw papers everywhere and knocked down chairs. After the counselors couldn't keep her calm or reach her mom, the administration decided to call school security to help settle her down. After school security could not handle her, the police were called to teach her a lesson. Though we (school personnel) thought this was a little excessive, we had no more say in the matter.

The police showed up, and the third grader would not cooperate, so the policeman decided to put her in handcuffs and transport her to juvenile—but not without a fight. When she was placed in the squad car, she kicked everything in sight.

As the officer took the report and she calmed down a little, he decided to open the door. The moment the door opened, she slipped her little hands out of the handcuffs and threw them at the officer. Before it was all said and done, the student reached under the officer's seat and snatched every cord loose to his computer, wreaking havoc on his system.

Lesson of the Day: Sometimes we can seek the wrong help for our students, and they become more problematic not only as kids, but as adults.

Reflection: There isn't a student out there who doesn't deserve the right to intervention before being placed in the custody of authorities. If counseling is needed, and a school counselor isn't the answer, then a clinical mental health counselor should be called in. Make sure you've exhausted all your resources and tried everything before calling the authorities (police). They should not be the first line of defense to bring about order, especially for an elementary student. In doing so, students become entangled with the justice system, therefore possibly giving them a permanent criminal conviction on their record before they have a chance to become mature adults who make sound decisions.

Not Right Now

The third grader came to my office really upset. He had gotten caught with a condom. I'm totally not making light of the matter; however, I couldn't stop staring at the condom wrapper. It had all types of passion fruit on it with coconut being the featured fruit. I was wondering where in the world it was purchased. He began to tell the principal the story of how somebody else had it and how they gave it to him.

As my principal listened to the student rant, he simply said to the young man, "Son, this is a good thing."

My eyebrows lifted about 2 inches. He continued to say, "This is good, **but not right now**! Maybe when you are of college age or older; however, not right now."

I thought that was profound advice. He didn't give him a long, drawn-out speech or ridicule him. He just told him "Not right now."

Lesson of the Day: Practical advice is sometimes the best advice.

Reflection: Although some may disagree, "keeping it real" with students today is the best way to go. With students being exposed to inappropriate social media, including music videos earlier and earlier, if we don't stop instances in their tracks, we will have a group of kids spreading negative behaviors like wildfire. If the behavior is serious enough, document it and inform parents, because it could be the beginning of conduct that needs more serious attention.

The Backpack

The grandfather ran up the hall asking me if I knew what class his granddaughter was in. He explained that his granddaughter had something in her backpack that belonged to him. After I found out who the teacher was, I escorted the grandfather to the child's class.

As the teacher, grandfather and I stood in the hall, he seemed relieved to get his hands on the backpack. He then proceeded to pull out the biggest bottle of gin. As my mouth flew open, I grabbed the grandfather's hand and told him not to pull out the bottle. I told him it was better if he just took the backpack home, and we would give the child something else to carry her books in.

Lesson of the Day: You simply don't learn how to deal with certain situations in college. Be prepared for anything.

Reflection: When dealing with situations that will leave you scratching your head, it is always a good practice to keep all comments to a minimum while staying professional. The real focus is on the students unless they appear harmed in any way. In this instance, the teacher was told to keep an eye out for the student and to report any changes in behavior, because alcoholism impacts the family as well as the individual.

102 Degrees

The child had a temperature of 102 degrees. We called her mother who lived in a nearby crime-ridden neighborhood. As she answered the phone, I could only hear her screaming, "Get down!" I asked the mother if everything was okay.

She informed me that she would come as fast as she could, however there was shooting going on outside of her window. I told her to please be careful, because I knew she had to walk to the school to pick up her child. All I could do was check on the student in the nurse's station and wait for her mom to pick her up.

Lesson of the Day: If most parents could provide better housing for their children, they would.

Reflection: It's okay to lend an ear when parents seem distressed. Most inner-city schools have a resource office that is equipped with a plethora of information about housing, educational opportunities, clothing, food, and other resources that can be beneficial for parents. These offices are more than happy to help parents, and need the help of referrals from teachers, social workers, counselors, and administrators to not only keep their programs running, but to get grants and donations from organizations that want to help parents thrive.

Alarm Clock

She was given an alarm clock to wake her and her kids up for school. The students had missed over 20 days during the first semester of school. There were times when they did come to school but would sit in the office well after dismissal waiting for her arrival. Many of those late days, their mother would come in reeking of alcohol and looking sleepy because she had passed out.

After meeting with the young mother of four about the absentees, the social worker asked her why she wasn't using the alarm clock that she so kindly bought her. The mom's response? "I don't have any batteries."

Lesson of the Day: Next time you try to give a parent an alarm clock, make sure it is electric. Leave room for no excuses.

Reflection: Some parents look at educators as nothing more than babysitters. They send students to school when it is convenient for them, and they keep students at home when it is convenient for them. In all instances, parents must be held accountable for getting their kids to school every day on time. Never be hesitant to call on the assistance of the attendance clerk and/or social worker. In most cases, they will try to work with the parents. However, in doing so, accept no poor excuses. If you must pair students up with a neighborhood buddy to help with accountability, do so. If you need to make a wake-up call, do so. Most students want to come to school. Give the students some of the responsibility, and they will rise to the occasion.

Rest in Peace

The sweet boy had ridden his bike to an afternoon church service for kids. During the Christmas Eve service, it began to storm with heavy winds. As he headed home in the heavy rain, in his pathway lay a hanging wire from a utility pole. Unbeknownst to him, it was a live wire.

When his bike came in contact with the wire, he was thrown off the bike while being electrocuted to death. He was in the fourth grade. The school was in complete disbelief...especially his classmates and teacher. The next day, we let balloons go in his honor and left flowers and stuffed animals at the site of the accident.

I counseled some of the students as they told me how nice he was and how much they missed him that day. The teacher knew that at any time she saw a hint of sadness from her students, my door was open for support and she could send them to me.

Lesson of the Day: Teach each student as if it were their last day.

Reflection: Losing a student is unimaginable and something that no teacher should experience. Sadly, death happens among our students, and one should have no time for regrets, just room for good memories. Good memories include knowing that you treated that student with dignity and respect, no matter their socioeconomic status. Good memories include knowing that you taught that student to the best of your ability, no matter their academic level. Also, counseling services are not only for students, but for the faculty as well. Most school healthcare plans for teachers provide for counseling sessions that do not require a referral and in most cases are free.

Moreover, know when tragedies happen, teachers and counselors must partner together to provide resources for students and families left to mourn.

The New Kid on the Block

She was a new teacher. Her make-up was pretty. She had a short jazzy haircut and olive skin with dark hair that gave her the appearance of a little French girl.

The first couple of weeks she tried very hard to adjust to the nature of her class. After several months, the pretty little French-looking girl was GONE. Her hair looked as though it were standing on top of her head, she wore no make-up, and she looked as pale as a ghost. She became known as the teacher who screamed at the top of her lungs.

The administration sent her to Classroom Management training and others helped to mentor her. Unfortunately, she didn't make it through the year. She turned in her resignation and never looked back.

Lesson of the Day: You can be the best at what you do, however in education, one size does not fit all.

Reflection: When all educators graduate from school, they are excited to set out and make their mark in the lives of students. In doing so, it's a good idea to be honest with yourself in deciding what population best fits your pedagogy. In most cases, a teacher's own educational upbringing shapes their expectations of student behavior, cognitive ability, and cultural views. When you are hired in a setting that doesn't fit your ideology, you either take on the "savior" attitude or you totally check out waiting for the school year to end; both being detrimental to students. It sends the message that inner-city students are unteachable, which couldn't be farther from the truth. In the end, find the placement that is best for you as an educator. You will do yourself and the students who you serve a favor.

Forty Dollars

He was in kindergarten and his coat was missing. After a few days, his mother came up to the school furious because it was told to her that another little boy in her son's class was wearing her child's coat. What could I do? I couldn't take the coat off the other little boy for him to freeze. This was a problem for the principal to handle.

As I told him the story, he said, "Sometimes some problems don't have to be a problem and aren't worth the hassle." He told me to come in his office and observe. As I followed him into the office where the mother was seated, she began to yell about the student wearing her son's coat and how she pays too much money for his clothes and how something should be done about the matter and how she didn't appreciate his coat being stolen and that her son had other coats but that wasn't the point.

My principal stopped her during her ranting by simply saying, "Ma'am, would you agree that if the student stole the coat, it's obvious he really needs one?"

She replied, "Yes."

Then, he proceeded to ask her, 'How much did you pay for the coat?"

She said, "About 30 dollars."

He said, “What if I gave you 40 dollars to buy another coat? Would that be okay with you?” As she calmed down, she said yes, while reminding us that she could buy him a new coat and repeating that was not the point. He reached in his pocket, gave her 40 dollars, and told her to have a nice day.

Lesson of the Day: Sometimes we must try different tactics to get different results.

Reflection: Although one may not agree with how the situation was handled pertaining to the stolen coat, good administrators know their parents and the potential for escalation in certain situations. It may not be the traditional way of handling incidents, but sometimes you do what works at that time. The end goal is to settle disputes while respectfully communicating with all who are involved. And while you may not handle another situation the same way, just know every problem has its individual solution.

The Microphone

Everyone loved to play with my plastic toy microphone. It wasn't fancy; however, students loved the sound of their echoed voice as they sang into it. One of my kindergarten students loved to come to my office. This particular day, she grabbed the microphone and began to play with it. So, I got engaged by asking her to sing her favorite song for me.

She began to sing a song, "I'm in love with the coco, I'm in love with the coco." I know you may have thought…hot cocoa, maybe even cocoa puffs. However, a few weeks ago I was invited to a party and the DJ played the very same song. After inquiring about the song at the party, I learned that the lyrics alluded to the love of cocaine.

I quickly told her the song was inappropriate and to sing another one. Let's just say, I had to take the microphone.

Lesson of the Day: You must stay current with young people by observing, listening, and asking questions. If not, you may entertain the insanity and not even know it.

Reflection: Lots of times, when you listen to music your body moves to the beat before your brain comprehends the words. In doing so, most lyrics bypass you. When you finally catch up with the lyrics, you are in disbelief and immediately change the station. As educators, we have the responsibility not to bring home into the school. We were hired to lead our students with good moral sense. Don't get caught up in a popularity contest normalizing inappropriate lyrics. Furthermore, the clean version doesn't always equate to "better" because of the context of the song. Offer your students an environment that reflects good, sound values and take teachable moments to talk about right and wrong choices because in some instances, they may not know the difference.

My Group

I noticed that several of my students had lost mothers and fathers, so I started a grief group. I followed a curriculum that focused on remembering your loved ones in different scenarios. However, one day I noticed most of my students crying because they missed the presence of their loved ones for various reasons.

I tried to address them all and before I knew it, I broke out into a song. The song was a popular nursery rhyme that came to mind about the rainbow. I don't know where that song came from, but I went with it.

It went:

"Red and yellow and pink and green, purple and orange and blue, you can sing a rainbow, sing a rainbow, sing a rainbow, too."

I sang it a few times and then had the students repeat after me. Before I knew it, we were all singing, and my students cheered up with smiles on their faces. After that day, during several sessions, my students requested that song, and they would draw the most beautiful rainbows.

Lesson of the Day: Sometimes you must leave the script and meet the immediate needs of your students.

Reflection: It's easy to follow a curriculum and even better, a pacing guide. However, what happens when your students aren't responding the way you planned? It is then that counselors, social workers, and teachers must be flexible. Be confident in yourself as a professional to know what's best for your students. If it means spending another week on a safety lesson and giving more examples than the curriculum provides, you must do so. Do what needs to be done for a successful outcome.

When in Doubt...Dance

I once had a student who could not get along with anyone in her class, partly due to her self-esteem. I must have met with her and five other girls from her class, every other week, to discuss issues concerning their friendship. After a while, it got really old and ugly.

Parents threatened other parents because of "she said/she said" and it was totally getting out of hand. Even the principal was at her wits' end, for the mother threatened to call the police or remove the student from the school each week.

Well, this went on for some time until one day, I had a session with the student and asked her if she had any friends that weren't in her class. She mentioned three girls from other classes. I coordinated the lunch times and had the girls meet on Fridays. During a couple of those sessions, we had pizza and danced.

This built her confidence and allowed her to express her real self with those who cared genuinely for her. I danced too, which gave the girls even more to giggle about. After several sessions, her mom calmed down a WHOLE lot and I continued to work on her daughter's self-esteem.

Lesson of the Day: Think outside the box. It may not be the conventional way, but don't give up.

Reflection: When setting up a comprehensive counseling program, it is important to include a developmentally appropriate curriculum that focuses on learning and behavioral goals. However, sometimes it's necessary to deviate from your systematic and planned program. Although you may not feel comfortable getting jiggy with it, there are times when students need to see the human, fun, down-to-earth side of you. It's amazing how just having a little fun with your students breaks down concrete barriers of communication. Afterward, when a sense of security is felt by your student, it is then that you can begin incorporating skills for success.

Adversity

A little kindergarten student came to me with tears in her eyes. She could barely speak English. She told me that the night before, her family was robbed as the gunmen put guns to her head, her baby brother's head, then to her mom's and her dad's heads. I was appalled and angry at how ruthless people could be.

I pulled that baby close to me and I told her that the people were bad, and they would be caught. I told her that she and her family didn't deserve it, and I was sure the police were doing everything they could to protect her family. My goal was to make sure that little student left my office feeling confident and at ease, knowing someone cared for her safety, that she would be okay and have a good school day.

After that day, I heard all too often how many of the Hispanic families were robbed because intruders knew they worked hard and kept cash on them. I felt hopeless, but I continued to support my students in every way that I could and believed that the authorities were doing their job.

Lesson of the Day: Adversity has no color. All races have struggles.

Reflection: Discrimination has no place in the school system. When a student comes to you in distress, it is your job, no matter their ethnicity, to comfort them on the spot and get to the bottom of it. In many instances, student discrimination leads to underachievement, lower attendance, and negative behavior. Your office/classroom should be a “Non-Judgment Zone.” Enhance your program by taking time to understand different cultures. Understanding people of different ethnicities will not only heighten your awareness but alleviate labeling and reduce prejudices.

Pride

I had two adorable little second graders who could not get along. I think the problem was, one was a little bit jealous of the other because she couldn't get her hair done as often and didn't have new clothes and shoes like the other little girl.

I began to meet with them on my lunch break every week, so they could get to know each other more. By the end of our sessions, they were best friends. However, I noticed that the one who was jealous had big, torn shoes flopping off her feet. So, naturally I went out and bought her two pairs of the cutest girly shoes I could find. I called her to my office and handed her the shoes.

She was so excited, she almost brought tears to my eyes. She asked if she could put one of the pair of shoes on as soon as I gave her the bag. I let her; however, I didn't throw away her old shoes, I gave them back to her to put in the bag.

The very next day, she came in with her other siblings and they told me, "Our parents want to talk to you!" I looked at my little student, wearing her old pair of shoes, with her head hanging down as she cried. I later called her to my office, and she said her mom and dad would not let her wear the new shoes and she had to bring them back to school. She also added that her parents said when those "big clown shoes" got too little, then she would get a new pair.

My heart just broke for the girl because I knew how badly she wanted to wear her new shoes and how she didn't feel like an outcast with them on. I finally asked her what she did with the new shoes, and before I knew it, our little lunch buddy, her now best friend, had them on.

Lesson of the Day: Not everyone who is down-and-out wants help. Some have too much pride, even if it means their loved ones go without.

Reflection: Don't take for granted that just because students come from a low socioeconomic background that it's okay to "sign them up." The proper thing to do is phone parents and talk to them personally so they hear the sincerity in your voice. When they feel as though you want to help their child from a place of kindness and not pity, they're more inclined to accept your assistance.

Reality

I will never forget this day. I really wanted one of my students to go on a field trip, and after several failed attempts to contact her mother, I decided to go to her house to obtain a permission slip. So, the teacher and I decided to ride over to the neighborhood of the community housing projects where 85% of our students lived. As I stepped out of the car, I looked around and it was as if everything was in slow motion… I saw stray dogs walking around, grown men standing around drinking, front yards with no grass, all while listening to gunshots.

My head was in a fog until I heard the happy screams of my name coming from students who recognized us. Still on our mission to get the permission slip signed, the teacher and I found the house and got what we came for. That day, my eyes were opened to the conditions and environment our students were brought up in and must endure before they even set foot in our school.

Although I don't want to be a crutch for my students, I empathize with them and have a better understanding of the shoes they must walk in.

Lesson of the Day: You must get background knowledge on your students to understand their experiences. In doing so, you should show empathy, which can eliminate obstacles and lead to accomplishments. Remember…all students have potential.

Reflection: Students are resilient. If you set high expectations for your students no matter their background, ethnicity, or socioeconomic state, they will flourish. However, it's important to know your students' environment and community so you can best support them at school. When you understand the dynamics of your students' home life, you can tailor and differentiate learning to assure that students perform at their highest potential.

Could You Walk in *Their* Shoes?

About the Author

Sharita Emerson Bell has been an educator for over 20 years. She served as a classroom teacher for 10 years, a school counselor for 8 years, and is currently a gifted and talented teacher. She has earned several awards throughout her career, including "Teacher of the Year."

As the child of a single parent, she experienced some perilous times of her own. Due to her own issues, she wasn't always an ideal student until one day when a fourth grade teacher took a personal interest in her behavior. From that day, she vowed to work with children and make it her mission to approach every student she meets, no matter their socioeconomic background, with love and respect. Her motto is, "Every child has potential."

Sharita earned her undergraduate degree from Tennessee State University along with a master's degree in education. She is also a certified school counselor. While at TSU, Sharita enjoyed being a member of the Aristocratic of Bands, T.E. Poag theatrical organization, and Delta Sigma Theta Sorority, Inc. She loves spending time with family and traveling. She has been married for 20 years and is the proud parent of a son.

www.ingramcontent.com/pod-product-compliance
Lightning Source LLC
Chambersburg PA
CBHW070937280326
41934CB00009B/1908
* 9 7 8 0 5 7 8 8 8 8 6 1 3 *